The Longest Walk Home:

How I Survived Teen Dating Violence

© 2019 by LaShonda Harolyn Henderson

Published by L&L Clinical Counseling Services, LLC

ISBN (Published): 978-1-7930-0578-6

Dedication

This book is dedicated to my two heavenly angels:

My mother, Linda McCrary, the woman who showed me unconditional love, and who has always been my number one fan.

My cousin, Johnella Singleton, who lost her life due to violence.

We speak your name.

I also dedicate this book to all survivors of domestic violence and those who have not yet found their strength to leave.

Contents

Acknowledgements

This book has been a source of my healing and ten years in the making. So, I first want to honor God for giving me the courage to finish what I started so long ago and for helping me see the value in my survival.

I would like to thank my parents: my father, Harold Henderson; and especially my mother, the late Linda McCrary Henderson. I thank you for loving me and ensuring that I knew I was born a queen. Thank you for those hard calls and the love you shared for me. Thank you for being my biggest fan. I love you.

I would like to thank my family for loving me unconditionally. Because of them I have the strength to carry on. A lot of who I am is because of who they are to me. I know this topic runs deep with my family and some are still hurting, so I acknowledge and honor your pain and your memories. I have been extremely blessed with a host of loving brothers and sisters, especially my maternal siblings (Dimitrich, Randy, Venecia, Deric, and Anwar) and my favorite cousin, Courtney. Thank you for being patient with me and putting up with my foolishness, whether you understood or not.

I would like to thank my Line Sisters (Dominique, Misti, and Valanda) for coming into my life when they did. God knew exactly what I needed and that meant the world to me. Special thanks to Misti Goodson, who stood by side every step of the way.

I would like to thank my high school best friends, Thalaria and Melissa. We did the best we could do with what we had, and we made the best or worst of it.

To my great friends I've met alone the way, Allecia, Easter, Jennifer and Tia; I thank you. Thanks for encouraging me on this journey. Thanks for being an ear when times were tough. Thank you for your constant prayers. Thank you for allowing me to be vulnerable. Even though you were not present through the abuse, you have held my hands through my healing process.

Thank you to all my supporters, sorority sisters and fraternity brothers, Facebook and Instagram friends, and anybody who has ever written an encouraging word, shared my work or wisdom, or donated time to helping me make things happen. I really truly appreciate you and none of this could not happen without you.

Introduction

The Longest Walk Home: My Journey of How I Survived Teen Dating Violence is a memoir of my life as a teenage victim of dating and domestic violence. I will take the readers on my personal journey; I went from being a blossoming, outgoing and outspoken girl to being in constant fear for my life at the hands of a young man who could only express his love for me through violence.

This is the story of a young girl who was exposed to dating violence at a young age. Trusting others and taking advice from the wrong people led to a decade of abuse. Just like the cycle of violence, my relationship went through the good and the bad, and near-death experiences, starting at the tender age of thirteen years old.

The message in this book is one of exposure. Dating violence can happen to the best of us. I've been facilitating group discussions with young men and women about teen/gender-specific issues for over twelve years; one common theme is teen dating violence. There is an overwhelming feeling that no one can stop the violence, no one understands the violence, and that no one else can relate to the pain.

There *is* life after an abusive relationship, and they need to hear and see it from someone who endured the violence for over a decade. *The Longest Walk Home* tells a story that will be familiar to women who have been victims of dating violence; it also speaks to the victims' families and friends.

I can tell this story because I have lived a life that others would have never imagined. I made a lot of mistakes because I felt sorry for myself. I thought that I deserved everything that happened to me. Then, I learned that this was not the case. I was not the only person experiencing this level of abuse. There were others who were also experiencing abuse, but it was hidden.

I hid the violence because I didn't want to be looked at as weak or be treated like a victim. I was indeed a victim; however, there was nothing weak about me. Everything was wrong and weak about my abuser.

LaShonda Henderson

Chapter 1

Loving Him . . . Like She Really Knew How

"She loved him, there was no question about that. But she loved him in a way he had yet to understand; yet, she loved him anyway." ~ J M Storm

---

was super excited about my ninth-grade year in high school. I had my high school career figured out already. I was going to play volleyball and basketball and be so great that I would land a college scholarship. I never thought that I would be interested in getting a boyfriend my freshman year; it just wasn't a priority for me.

I just wanted to be happy and free from the anger that I carried for so long due to the harsh realities that I was dealing with. My past traumas had me behaving in ways that I didn't understand at that moment.

I had a rough childhood. It began with the divorce of my parents. I completely felt abandoned by my father. He relocated away from our city, and my contact with him became so infrequent that I didn't know when I would see him again. My wondering stopped when he stopped showing up. At that time, my aunt and cousins lived in our home so we were basically raised as siblings. There were nights that I witnessed my aunt being physically abused by her boyfriend. I would wake up to her screaming, and after witnessing several incidents of domestic violence, I started fighting with my aunt's boyfriend, even grabbing a knife to protect her from him.

That was a crazy time in my life. The only consistent man in my life at that time was my oldest brother, Dimitrich (Deek), who was murdered on Memorial Day when I was twelve years old. To say the least, I was devastated. He left to get ice for a family cookout, and my mom got a call stating that he had been shot. Later, we were told that he died. I was angry, confused, and felt helpless. I was unsure about who I was and where my life was headed. I really couldn't see the brightness in any day.

Hear me out! I was abandoned by my father; witnessed violence in my home; and was traumatized by the murder of my oldest brother, all before I was thirteen years old. Now here I am, almost fourteen, entering high school with no real expectations other than wanting to play basketball and volleyball, and to graduate.

Two months after school started, I was informed that someone on the bus that I rode to school "liked" me. I think initially I was like, "*Oh, okay,*" and I brushed it off. Later, I began to like the idea that someone liked me. We finally spoke (his name was Six); and eventually started sitting together on the bus. We lived in the same neighborhood. We really didn't talk that much because we both were quite shy. On Halloween, I went to his house with my best friend. Six and I decided that we would become boyfriend and girlfriend.

We became inseparable. When we were not at basketball practice, we were together. He wanted all of my free time. I wanted to give it all to him, and I never thought anything about it. Within three months, we started having sex

It was a normal Sunday afternoon for me. I was getting dressed to go to a Junior Temple meeting when I heard a knock at the door. It was my boyfriend. He wasn't his normal happy-to-see-me self. He came inside. We sat on the couch in near silence as I put on lotion. I got up to get my pantyhose, and when I sat down to put them on, he asked me who went with me to the county fair. I responded that I took my nephew to the fair. Before I could ask him why he was asking, he slapped me very hard on the face. Initially, I was in shock. I began to cry.

Moments later, I went to my room, but my mom yelled out for me to hurry so that we could leave. He just sat in the living room, like nothing happened, and eventually left the house without saying a word to me. My mother and I got in the car and left for my youth meeting. I never said a word.

A few days passed without us speaking. He then called. He told me that his cousins said that they saw me at the fair with a guy. He apologized and said he would never hit me again. I had no reason to apologize, so I didn't. Someone lied about me. He told me that he loved me and didn't want to lose me. I told him that if he ever put his hands on me again, we would break up and I would tell my mother.

Although we got past that incident and pretended like it never occurred, I knew that it was not going to be the last time. He became very controlling and started to embarrass me in front of his friends by demanding all my attention. He wasn't paying any attention to me. He wanted to have his eyes on me and know exactly what I was doing at all times.

Chapter 2

Pregnant and Fifteen

"With a secret like that, at some point the secret itself becomes irrelevant. The fact that you kept it, does not." ~ Sara Gruven

---

After the aggression became more consistent, my life became a little overwhelming. I tried to balance my relationship, school, and playing sports. We were near one another about twelve hours a day. We rode the bus, attended the same school, played sports afterschool, and were together for hours after our basketball practices. I felt suffocated, but not enough to break it off with him.

Well, it was no time before I received my first black eye. Everything with him was a surprise; I never saw it coming. He would push or slap me because someone (another boy) looked at me. (Like I had control of who looked at me.) I used to think I was a tough girl, but he constantly reminded me that I wasn't tough at all.

On this particular day, I was sitting on a corner near my house with some of my friends from our neighborhood. We were just hanging out and acting silly. I remember laughing loudly at something one of my friends said. My back was turned away from the eastside of the street, and out of nowhere Six abruptly walked up. In front of everyone, he punched me in the eye, knocking me to the ground. Not a single word was said. Everyone around me was shocked because they hadn't seen it coming, either; but nobody uttered a single word. As hard as I tried to save face and act unaffected, I couldn't. I became very tearful and confused about why I was just attacked. It took my friends a few minutes to comfort me. To be honest, I was more upset with them for just standing around and doing nothing, more than I was upset with Six for attacking me.

All I thought was, *How am I going to hide this?* My eye became bruised immediately. I can recall my brother, who is eleven months older than I, saying, "I'm going to tell Mom!" I begged him not to, but I also refused to speak to my boyfriend again. This was getting out of control. I never knew what to expect. I didn't even see him getting upset. If he felt that he had a reason to hit me, he never told me the reason. I didn't understand how someone could say they loved you in one breath, and in the next breath, treat you like some man on the street. I'm not even sure that he would have done what he did to me, to a man on the street.

For a week, I walked around wearing dark sunglasses. My sister was trying to find remedies to get my eye to go down, but it didn't work. My mom found out that Six blacked my eye and she called his parents. And yes, my brother, told her because he got upset with me.

At the request of my mother, Six and his parents came to my house to discuss the incident. I really wanted to stay in my bedroom, but my mother made me come out so that his parents could see my face and hear what their son had done to me. His parents claimed that they didn't know where he learned these behaviors, but my mother wasn't having it. My mother knew that he didn't just wake up and decide to beat up on me. She knew that a young man his age had either been a victim or witness to domestic violence in his home or family. Mom ordered Six to never come to the house again and said that I could not ever speak with him again. We followed Mom's orders for about three weeks. Although my mother forbade us to be together, we saw each other daily when she left for work, and every day after the summer work program.

Our relationship intensified and we began having sex. Six was my first love. Time passed and so did my period. I began to feel tired and I started gaining a little weight. My sister detected that I was possibly pregnant. I asked my sister how she knew and she asked why I wanted to know. I told her the truth; my period was late. My brother walked into the room, and heard us talking. He asked if I was pregnant. I denied it and told him not to say anything. He promised he wouldn't. My sister and her friend took me to get a pregnancy test. I'll be damned; I was pregnant and fifteen.

I took pills that were supposed to terminate the pregnancy. When they didn't work, I told Six. He wasn't excited or nervous. I knew my mom was not going to be happy. She had already told me to never see him again, so how the heck was I going to explain to her that I was pregnant. *This would not end well,* as I thought to myself.

After more than a week passed, my brother and I got into another argument. He kicked me in the side, and I threw a pair of scissors at him, hitting him in the back. His next move ruined my day. Yelling and hollering, he said, "I'm gonna tell Ma that you're pregnant!" And, then he did! Next thing I heard was my mom calling me. "Shonda, get your ass in here, NOW!" My cover was blown. She knew I was pregnant. She knew I did exactly what she told me not to do … I continued to see Six behind her back, had sex, and got pregnant.

The next few weeks were quiet and awkward. My mom said little to nothing to me, and my brother laughed at the awkwardness that he created by letting the secret out. One day, my mom came home and said, "Let's go." I inquired about where we were going, but she told me to "shut the hell up." We pulled up to this building and people were outside holding signs and shouting. I didn't know exactly why we were there, but I knew it was a place for pregnancy testing and other services. She took me to get an abortion. Was I mad? Not at all. What was I going to do with a baby at fifteen? I thought about the fact that I was carrying the child of a boy who had no hesitation about abusing me. After I told Six about the procedure, he immediately came to my house. We quietly sat on the sofa pretending to watch television. My abortion became a secret among a handful of people. Other than Six, I only told my immediate family and two friends.

Chapter 3

Hiding Behind the Shades

"She was brave and strong and broken all at once." ~ Anna Funder

There was never a dull moment dating my boyfriend. No one saw it because he was a jokester, and a star athlete.

I would cover the bruises with long sleeve clothing or makeup. I never wore makeup, but mom and sister did. I would sneak into their stash and use it to hide the bruises. As soon as I applied the makeup, I would sweat and the makeup would run.

I tried not to get dressed in front of friends or teammates so that they wouldn't see the marks on my arms or back. And when they did notice the bruises, I would blame them on falling or bumping into things because I was clumsy. Truthfully, I was falling due to his punches and kicks.

Time passed and my senior year began. Six was a year ahead of me so he was now in college. Although we were apart, we continued to date. Six wasn't even physically located in the same city, but I continued my life as though he was. When we talked on the phone, he made me aware that he knew my every move. I knew his friends and family members were giving him daily updates about me, he had someone watching me at all times.

Homecoming weekend finally arrived. I should have been excited because I was in the running for homecoming queen. Instead, I was worried. I knew that Six was trying to come home for the celebration. Thankfully, it was looking like he wouldn't be able to make it.

I was at my Godmother's home getting dressed for the homecoming game. I just knew the night was going to be awesome, regardless of whom would be named homecoming queen, because I didn't think Six would be in town. I was crowned homecoming queen! It was one of my best days and nights of my high school life. Well, unbeknownst to me, Six was at the homecoming game. Even with me being crowned queen, it still wasn't enough to make him happy. He jumped the gate to get into the game, and it was all my fault. He made sure that I was miserable for the entire weekend. I didn't dare talk to anyone in his presence because I knew what the outcome would be.

When I was finished dancing with the homecoming king, I could see the anger in Six's eyes. I knew that after the dance I would pay big time. And, I did! I just wanted the weekend to be over, so that he could return to college. I wanted to go back to being a normal high school senior, without him unnoticeably walking up on me. At this point, I thought my secret was out. To my surprise, no one said anything about it.

Chapter 4

Enough Is Enough . . . Well, Not Really!

"He who knows that enough is enough will always have enough." ~ Lao Tzu

t was Martin Luther King Jr. Day, and I was getting ready to head to the parade. Six was adamant that I come to his house prior to heading to the festival in the park, which was held immediately following the parade.

When I arrived at his house, Six was sitting in the living room waiting. I knew something was off, but I didn't know what was in store for me. He asked me if I was seeing someone else. I answered, "No!" Before I could say another word, he hit me in my face with a basketball, over and over again. When I attempted to get up, he started punching me. He said that if I moved; it would only get worse. I balled up in a corner, covered my face, and cried. He continued to bounce the ball off my back. Then, he finally stopped. I got up, thinking it was over, and then he started punching and kicking me in the face, head, stomach, and whatever he could reach. I knew I needed to get out or I wouldn't live through the attack. When he turned his back, I ran towards the front door. He blocked the door and wouldn't let me out as I begged and screamed for help. After slapping and spitting in my face, he finally moved out of the way. I ran to my aunt's house and told her what happened. My aunt called out to police officers who were on bikes, patrolling our neighborhood. I told the police what happened to me. They went looking for him, but Six was gone. They came back and completed the paperwork needed to file charges. Later, I learned that Six's best friend's mom, who was employed by the state attorney's office, had the report come up missing. No charges were ever filed and I didn't hear from him for months.

Chapter 5

For Better or Worse

> *"Take each other for better or worse, but not for granted."* ~ Arlene Dahl

graduated high school and earned a college basketball scholarship. I had to leave for college early to start physical conditioning for the basketball season. I was not in constant contact with Six; however, we occasionally spoke.

College life was good. No one knew me or knew about what I had endured. And, I didn't care to share. This was my opportunity for a fresh start. I met young, brilliant women, like me, who loved basketball. I found myself being drawn to children, so when I was not in class or at an away game, I volunteered as a mentor at a local elementary school.

One day, I called home to check in with my family, particularly my cousins. I received a message to call Six. Apparently, he had been asking about me. I contemplated calling him, but I did. He was heading out and said that he would call later. And he did! We talked and caught up over the phone. He said he missed me and wanted to visit me at college. I must admit that I had mixed feelings about him visiting for several reasons. I wondered if he had changed. I wondered how he would respond to me and my new male friends from the basketball team. We all lived in the same complex and were basically a big family.

Well, the day arrived that Six came to visit. All was fine until one of my teammates came to the door. I introduced my teammate to Six, and then he left. Six became upset and wanted to go for a walk. He wanted to isolate me from the others.

As we were walking, he slapped my face and accused me of dating one of the players. I denied his accusation and accused him of dating someone at his college because I had never given him any indication that we were still dating. The night ended horribly. It was nothing like the good time, I had imagined it would be. He left to go to his aunt's house, who lived in my college town. Later, he returned to his college in Orlando. There was no apology nor any goodbyes. I didn't answer any of his calls or attempt to talk with him. As the school semester came to a close, Six and I talked and decided that when we returned home that we would date again.

It was a Friday night at home, and someone hosted a party at the local women's club. I went to the party and met up with my best friend. Six came to the party with his family. Throughout the evening, Six's cousin kept telling me that Six wanted to talk. I went outside only to find out that Six didn't want me; his cousin was only playing around. After the third time, I refused to go outside again. So this time, Six came and got me. When we were outside, I explained to him why I hadn't come to see what he wanted. A neighborhood friend interrupted our conversation. Our friend spoke with us, and then asked me questions about my older brother. Before the guy walked away, Six punched me in the eye so hard that I thought I had whiplash. I screamed. The friend that brought me to the party was trying to take me home in her mom's car. But, Six jumped in too. He punched and pinched me in the back seat. I took out a key ring with a blade on it and cut him on his arm.

When we got home, I ran into the house and locked the door to keep Six out. He stayed outside my room window the entire night, begging me to come out to talk with him. The next morning, I came outside with a knife to protect myself. I told Six that our relationship was over and not to contact me again. Again, he apologized. But, I was not trying to hear it.

I was so done with him. Well, that was until he called a few months later. While coming from the club, he informed me that he joined the military. He wanted me to marry him. I said, "You are joking?"

Then, I asked him what happened to school and his scholarship. He simply said that he decided to leave school to join the Navy. I told him to call me the next day when he was sober.

As I was walking out the door for practice, my phone rang. It was Six. He asked me again to marry him before he left for basic training. I agreed, but told him that I had to ask my mother. I ended the call with him and called my cousin. I wanted her to call and ask my mom if I could get married. My cousin made a three-way call, but my mother didn't know that I was on the phone. My mother went off and told my cousin not to call her with foolishness. So, basically, the answer was *no*.

I knew that my mother didn't approve of me getting married; however, Six and I set a date for me to come home so that we could go to the courthouse, anyway. I caught a Greyhound bus home and we got married the next day. Two days later, Six left for the military, and I left our marriage certificate on a table before heading back to college.

When I returned to college, my basketball coach was waiting for me at the Greyhound station. My roommate was the person who was supposed to pick me up. However, the coach told me that my mom had been calling every hour on the hour. He asked if it was true that I got married. I denied it. Coach said, "It must be true; you are wearing a wedding ring." I was busted! When I got to my room, I immediately called my mom who said that she had been calling nonstop for the past six hours.

My mom was not happy. She told me that all she knew was that I better graduate from college, and it didn't make sense to run off and get married. Despite her feelings, I thought my marriage was perfect. Perfect, since I was in Florida and he was in Chicago. He was in training, and all our conversations were limited because of his time restraint

Chapter 6

Hiding My Tears

"Forgive me if I smile, it's just to hide my fears. Forgive me if I laugh, it's just to hide my tears." ~ Unknown

---

Months passed and I didn't see Six until his graduation day. After that, I didn't see Six again for three months because he had to complete another training. Meanwhile, I signed another scholarship at the Florida Institute of Technology, which was closer to home.

While at FIT, I played basketball and enjoyed my college life while he was in training. When Six returned home, he informed me that we had to move to Virginia. My basketball coach and mother didn't agree. They felt that I should remain at FIT to finish school. I disagreed. I was super excited because he appeared to be a changed man. We were starting a new life and things were looking up for us.

I found a college in Virginia called Old Dominion University, and got accepted. By the end of the year, we moved to Virginia Beach, Virginia. Six was all that I had in Virginia because I had no friends nor family close. He had a military family, but I only had him. Since we depended on one another, we did not argue as much. We only had one car, so transportation was limited for me. On the days, I had classes at ODU's satellite campus in Virginia Beach, I drove him to work. When I didn't have class, I stayed at home. That was until I got a job.

I was really excited to get a job so that I could meet people. Along the way, I gained some independence, which he frowned upon. I really wanted a social life. Although I met one person, she had a baby and really couldn't hang out. The following spring, I began taking classes at the main campus in Norfolk. I was able to meet classmates and hang out during the activity hour. In class, I met a young woman who was a member of Zeta Phi Beta Sorority, Incorporated. She invited me to attend a sorority interest meeting. From there, I started meeting more people and felt like I found my strength. Meanwhile, Six constantly reminded me that he was in control. I quit my job in Virginia Beach because we moved to Norfolk.

After long days and nights, I finally became a member of Zeta Phi Beta Sorority, Incorporated and my life was full and hopeful again. I was going to school, working, doing community service, and going to parties, all of which were a no-go in his eyes.

Six decided that I needed a pager so that he would always have access to me. When he paged me, I didn't answer. I knew I would get beat up that night or day. One time, I didn't answer my pager because I was five minutes away from home. When I arrived home, he assaulted me and the pager got damaged. Six lost control and destroyed the pager. Since I no longer had a pager, Six couldn't reach me. Breaking the pager was the best thing that happened to me. After this incident, Six never knew where I was because I could no longer be reached. Karma at work!

Chapter 7

———∽∾∽———

Telling My Secret

"When you stand and share your story in an
empowering way, your story will heal you
and your story will heal somebody else."
~ Iyanla Vanzant

landed a job as a residential counselor at a high-risk girl's program. I worked with girls in the child welfare system who suffered from a variety of mental illnesses and behavioral issues. Due to the severity of their mental illnesses, only four girls resided in the group home. Working at the group home was a breath of fresh air. I formed a connection with the thriving young ladies, all of whom fought for my attention. Serving as a role model and mentor motivated me to look at my own life. There, I had an opportunity to encourage change in the lives of these girls; yet, I carried a deep, dark secret. I was being abused by the very person who promised to protect and love me.

Going to work each day was an escape from my reality. Nightly, I stayed up talking about college, boys, and the rest of the world. I was 21 years old and they were 17... not that much of an age difference... but they had their full lives ahead of them. I began to think that *I needed to change my life, or my secret would only get worse.*

I remember inviting my line sisters (the ladies I completed the intake process with for Zeta) to my apartment and I prepared crab legs for them. We loved crab legs and Red Lobster. We talked about our futures and I recall saying, "I'm not going to be in this situation much longer if some things don't change."

Meanwhile, I did as much as my single line sisters because I demanded my independence. Ultimately, it resulted in a lot of fights with Six. I never initiated any of the fights. But, when we did fight, I would cover my face because I knew his goal was to black my eye to isolate me. I would just ball up and cover my face. Well, I shared my real life with my line sisters and a coworker, who was much older. My coworker was a librarian who worked part-time at the group home.

After I shared what I was going through, she immediately became my advocate. If she hadn't heard from me, she would call me or pop up at my apartment. If he was home, she would be as cool as a button. She would say, "I've been off work for days, and I wanted to say hello to you since I was in your neighborhood." Even though I had a cell phone and a house phone, she would just pop up ... just because.

Although she never encouraged me to leave, she always encouraged me to be safe. Her advice was for me to learn what triggered Six, and to learn not do it. At this time, Six and I had been together for nearly six years. I thought I knew him and his triggers, but they changed. He was no longer the tenth grader that I dated. She would say, "If you plan on leaving, be smart about it. Don't threaten to leave, but when you are ready, just leave."

I can't lie, I felt vulnerable. So many people (five) knew what I was enduring. I believed that I was viewed as strong and capable. After my discloser, I felt like I was a weak woman.

Chapter 8

The Good in Goodbye

"When you're holding on to someone that you gotta let go.

Someday you'll see the reason why sometimes, yeah sometimes, there's a good in goodbye." ~ Carrie Underwood

One night when Six was on duty, my sorority sisters and I went to a campus Webb Jam, a dance party. Six had to stay on the ship. So, since he had broken my pager, he had no way of contacting me if I wasn't home. I came home about 2 a.m. and noticed that there were two missed calls from Six. I had no worries because he knew I was going to the Webb Jam.

To my surprise, he came home early in the morning, and asked me about the party the previous night. Before I could get a word out, he knocked me into a wall with one punch. Then, it was punch after punch, and kick after kick. I was accustomed to his beatings; I always knew to cover my face. Other than the MLK Day hostage incident, that morning was the longest time he beat on me. And this time, it came with threats that he would kill me if I reported it to his command. After that ordeal, I was basically made to undress and have sex with him. I did.

After he fell asleep, rage took over my body and mind. I had thoughts of him trying to kill me the next time, or worse, me killing him. I was not going to be beaten any longer and then made to have sex with the person who had been abusing me for years. All morning, I tossed and turned. I had to be at work at 4 p.m. so I finally got out of bed. I called my line sister to meet me at her favorite Chinese restaurant.

While in the shower, I observed the bruises on my body. I checked the mirror and my back was just as bad as the front. More thoughts in my head, came up. As I cried, I thought to myself, "*This is it. I'm done.*" I was convinced that either I was going to die, or I was going to kill him. I didn't want either of those outcomes. So, I got dressed and left the apartment.

As planned, I met with my line sister. I shared with her what had occurred that morning and showed her my back. She stated that she would ask her mom if I could come stay with them until graduation.

I headed to work, and she called me later to tell me that her mother said I could sleep in their enclosed sun porch. I was happy. Although when I went to work, I could barely move. I was in so much pain.

Chapter 9

Loving Me Never Felt So Good

---

*"When I accept myself, I am freed from the
burden of needing you to accept me."*
~ Dr. Steve Maraboli

Being able to see and think clearer was what I was most excited about. But living with someone other than my husband bought unexpected fears. In my mind, I started to prepare how my day-to-day life would look, including living in someone else's home.

I had it planned perfectly; I would pack little by little over the next couple of days. When he left for work, I would be gone. As the third day approached, we barely communicated. I did not give him any indication that I was done. It was all a plot in my mind until it became reality. He finally left.

I packed the truck and left. He did not have a clue where I went. I'm not sure if he initially cared that I left. I moved in with my line sister and her family, and sharing a space with Sparky, their dog, wasn't bad at all. I had a better relationship with Sparky than I had with my husband.

My routine became normal: class, sorority functions, work, and home. During this time, my life was predictable and my only real concern was me. My immediate goal was to get out of this marriage alive so that I could graduate, and move back home.

I focused on school, work, and the sorority. Much of my time was spent thinking about what I would tell my family when they asked why I was back home and not with my husband. I created stories and practiced lies to tell.

I began to appreciate and value the work I was doing with the girls at the group home. I took them on various outings including walks on the beach and on-campus tours of a college campus and its activities. On a daily basis, I heard them say things like, "I want to be like you when I grow up." This made me re-think my desire to return home to Florida. When we went to the beach, we would meditate. I took time to talk with God and time to reflect about my next moves. I knew I could not remain living with my line sister. I was always hypervigilant. However, the environment that I helped create for the girls at the group home was a safe haven. It also made me feel safe and I could let down my guard. Why? Six did not have any idea where the group home was located.

By this time, we had two cars. I was working in Portsmouth so Six never had to drive me to work. Days turned into weeks, and I began getting phone calls. I didn't answer. Well, initially, I didn't answer the calls, but I later became annoyed and picked up. On the phone was his family asking me to return home to work things out. Of course, I said, "No!" or that "I would think about it." But, they were just thoughts.

Some nights I stayed at the group home. I knew that my husband would never show up and I just needed some time to be alone. The average person would be upset to stay at work, but not me. I enjoyed being where I was appreciated. I enjoyed being where I could be me ... a leader, and an inspiration to the young and vulnerable. But, I too was young and vulnerable. When I left the group home to go to class or my line sister's house, I would always think about my next move. I chanted, "*I must pass this semester. I must make money. And, I must get myself out of this situation alive.*"

By this time, the girls at the group home would ask me why I wouldn't leave and why they hadn't met my husband. The reality was I didn't want them to know. I made up good excuses to tell them. I really didn't want them to know that I was being abused.

Here, I was helping the girls work on their own wounds, and I was the one hiding. I couldn't let them know that I was broken and battered. They loved who they thought I was. Well, I really was all that they thought I was; however, I was being tormented. I had to get out of my situation before they learned about my truth in the news. My focus shifted to repairing how I viewed myself and how I could keep myself out of harm's way.

Chapter 10

Easier Said Than Done

"Be sure to taste your words before you spit them out." ~ *Unknown*

Nearly a month had gone by since the day I left. This meant that I was only a few months away until my graduation. It felt like I was settled mentally, but definitely not physically. I missed my own space and my own boundaries. I missed them both, but not enough to turn back. I was talking to my mom daily and the rest of my family weekly. I was preparing to return to Florida, thus leaving Virginia behind.

After work one night, I received a call from Six. I was very reluctant to answer his call because I wasn't sure how the conversation would go. When I mustered the courage to answer, I answered to a very shaken and humble voice. He asked how I was doing and made small talk about school, work, and family. Perhaps, we got in one good laugh before he asked if I would meet him in person to talk. I told him that I didn't think it was a good idea because he was unpredictable. I never knew what to expect. Besides, he previously threatened me with death, so I was not interested in meeting him anywhere.

After 30 more minutes, I agreed to meet him in a public location within the next few days. I had a few sleepless nights because I thought about what the meeting would look like and its potential outcomes. I was nervous. Would our meeting be violent? Would it end with him being arrested? On the contrary, I was also hopeful.

On the day of our meeting, I arrived in a public parking lot. To my surprise, he was already there. He asked me to come to his car, but I told him to get into my truck. I didn't want to put myself in an unsafe position, where I could possibly be kidnapped or assaulted. I just thought being in my truck would be safer.

Initially, we sat and talked about school, work, my sorority happenings, and then us. He told me that he missed me and that things hadn't been the same since I left. We had a lot of quiet moments filled with awkward stares. Nothing he said encouraged me to go back.

Chapter 11

Graduation in Sight

---

*"You can never cross the ocean unless you have
the courage to lose sight of the shore." ~
Unknown*

Two weeks passed since Six and I met face-to-face. I woke up early and decided to take a ride to our apartment. I parked in a lot that was three building away from our building. My goal was to be discreet so that neither Six nor his friends would see my truck.

When I entered the apartment, it was a mess. It looked like it was abandoned. I searched for supplies to clean the apartment as though I was living there again. As I cleaned, I had so many mixed emotions. I felt guilty for abandoning my husband and for not fulfilling my vows as a wife. Although he was very abusive to me, I felt lost. I missed being in my own space; awkward moments of laughter and silence; and his friends' voices when they came to visit. After all, his friends made him happy. I also missed cooking him my two favorite meals. Hell, I just missed what was my normal for so many years.

I continued to clean. First, the living room. Then, the kitchen. Next, the bedroom. I also washed all the dirty laundry. I then decided that I wouldn't neglect the duties of a wife. I went grocery shopping so that I could cook him dinner. Not once did I consider that he could come home, and find me cleaning and cooking.

I didn't think about what I would say or do. Or what he would say or do?

When I returned to the apartment complex, I scanned the lot for his car. It was not there. I cooked dinner and quickly left. I was not ready to have a conversation with him. However, my actions revealed that I really missed being home.

Later that afternoon, Six called to ask if I would come home to have dinner with him. I replied, "No!" I really needed to finish studying before I headed to work. He, then thanked me for dinner, and asked if he could visit me at work. I told him that he couldn't come to my job because it would violate patient confidentiality. We talked for a few minutes more and I said, "I will talk with you soon." The called ended with him saying that he loved and missed me.

The rest of my evening was preoccupied with thoughts of returning home as well as thoughts of blame and shame. Why would I allow myself to be placed back in this situation? I've opened back up the doors to communication. Why did I give him false hope? Or was it false hope? I missed being in my comfort zone and made excuses about why it wasn't so bad to be back home.

One week passed, and I was roughly one month from graduation. I decided to go back home. In my head, I was thinking that this might be the wakeup call that he needs. I thanked my line sister and her mother for allowing me to stay in their home, and of course, they said I could always return.

During my first week back, things seemed normal. We talked minimally, but there was no arguing. We continued with our daily schedules. I went to school and work, and did sorority stuff. He went to work and hung out with his friends. But, one Saturday morning, I stayed home to clean and research new potential job opportunities. After all, I was a soon-to-be college graduate. I was playing Betty Wright's, "No Pain, No Gain" when I got a call from my oldest brother's girlfriend. The talk with her provided me a moment to reflect on the past few months and the opportunity to catch up with her. I told her how things were going, and that Six and I were pretty much walking on egg shells around each other. I didn't want to upset him to the point that he would hit me, and he didn't want to upset me to the point that I would leave again. As I sat on the couch laughing, I heard loud music outside. I looked out the window and saw that it was Six and his friends. For about five minutes, they sat in the car. Then, Six came inside.

When he entered the apartment, I knew that he wasn't expecting me to be home. He thought that he would be hanging out with his friends alone. He paced a little as I continued to talk on the phone. Finally he said, "You are not going to do anything with yourself today." And, then the arguing began. My brother's girlfriend remained on the phone just in case she needed to call the police. My gut told me that he wouldn't hit me since his friends were outside. But, I was not taking any chances. He said very mean things to me, including, "You can pack your stuff up and leave if you want to."

Months prior to me moving out, I went to the doctor to get a birth control shot. I didn't want to end up pregnant. He had no clue that I had done this. This wasn't my first time on birth control since we got married. I kept forgetting to take the pills. Therefore, I opted for the birth control shot. I wasn't going to run the risk of getting pregnant.

Despite this fact, my body didn't respond very well to the shot. I was so sick that I couldn't walk for three days. The worst part of it all was that I was on my cycle every day. He was yelling and calling me all kinds of names, except a child of God. He then stated that I needed to take my ass to the doctor because there was something wrong with me since I was bleeding every day. I was shocked because he previously didn't voice his concerns about my bleeding frequency. So out of frustration, the secret I was keeping from him came out. I told that I was bleeding because of the birth control that I was taking, and that I wanted to ensure that I didn't get pregnant and bear a child from his jealous ass. At that point, the arguing stopped. I dodged an object that he threw at my head. Then, he immediately left the apartment. In that moment, I knew that our marriage was not meant to be. Instead of moving out, I planned another exit strategy.

I spoke with a coworker who knew about my situation. She advised me to be very safe. I told her that I was just going to move back to Florida. I wasn't trying to stay in Virginia. She invited me to stay in her home until I graduated or found another job to support myself. I called my mother to inform her about the occurrence. Mom told me that I just needed to come home. She said that when she came for graduation that we would pack my things and I would return with her. But, I wanted out immediately. The day after my last final exam, I planned to pack my truck to leave.

Chapter 12

Regaining My Strength

"Do not drown in your own emotions. Take a breather, regain your strength, do not let what worries you, control you" ~ Leon Brown

On the following Saturday, I was done for good. I didn't care about walking across the stage to receive an empty envelope. I knew that degrees would be mailed. I told Six that I was leaving him and going back to Florida. He told me that he received military orders deploying him to the Mediterranean for six months. From my lens everything, including the stars, were aligning. Therefore, my exit would not be so dramatic.

He asked me if I was sure this is what I wanted to do, and I stated, "Yes, I can't live like this anymore." He stated that he was not going to force me to stay. That week was emotionally rough. I cried a lot, and I pushed through my decision to leave. Six was leaving for his tour in a month. All I had to do was pack my clothing and items I accumulated since being in college.

I finally completed all of my finals. I called one of my professors to ensure that I earned the grade I desired. The professor told me that I did and that he hoped that I would apply for graduate school. I told him that unfortunately I was in a very violent marriage, and was leaving for Florida the next day. He was disappointed, but wished me well.

By 5 a.m. the next day, my truck was all packed and I was on my way to Florida.

The drive home was horrible. I was worried about all the questions I would have to answer from family and friends. I practiced what I would say to whomever, and thought about what I was going to do with myself. I went to Florida with no job and no plans of getting one any time soon.

When I arrived home, I parked my truck in the backyard to avoid people. I didn't want to answer questions about why I was home without my husband. Only a few close friends and family knew that I returned. Days quickly turned into weeks, and I continued to lay around the house. I felt the ease of depression. So, I pushed myself. I knew that I needed to get my life together. *This is not what my life was meant to be like, and this is not going to be the story of my life*. I started exercising and reconnected with family and friends. I had been gone for more than four years. They gave me the strength to move forward.

Then, the day I was trying to avoid happened. Six's father came to my house. He saw my truck in the driveway. He knew I was home because Six told him I was there. He told me that he knew that Six and I were not together. He told me that I should pray while Six is out to sea. He said I should ask God to heal and restore our relationship. That was not what I wanted to hear or do. Out of respect, I agreed to do so. He then told me that Six asked if he could call me to talk. I told him that Six could call, but I wasn't going to talk about reconciliation. He smiled and stated that it was going to take some time, and this time apart could improve our relationship. Six and I had basically been together since we were 13 years old.

The next day Six called. We talked briefly. We talked about how his first tour was going and how I felt being home again. We didn't discuss our relationship. After that conversation, we talked several times a month for nearly three months. I decided that I was going to join the military because I wanted to leave Florida. When we discussed my decision to join, Six was not happy. But, he said if that is what I wanted to do; he was okay with it. I knew I didn't need his approval.

Chapter 13

Army Strong

"Sometimes you don't realize your own strength until you come face to face with your greatest weakness." **~ Susan Gale**

---

thought joining the military would pull me from the stagnation of being at home, I thought it would free me from the loneliness and the shame that I carried about being at home. I was supposed to test for Officer Candidate's School, but I was too impatient to wait out the process. Therefore, I joined the Army Reserve as a military police officer. Out of all the occupations I could choose, why did I choose military police? Apart of me thought that I could rebuild my strength. I wanted to get stronger physically; and learn to be more assertive and independent. That's what I wanted to gain.

It was August when I left for basic training. I was headed to Missouri. The moment I stepped off the plane, I began to regret my decision to join. For so long, I was bossed around. Why would I agree to be told what to do for the next four months? I immediately begin to beat myself up with negative self-talk.

I saw myself, yet again, making a horrible decision. I questioned the decisions to leave my ex and to leave my mother, who had just gotten used to me being back home. For the first month away, I cried every night. My mother asked me not to call her anymore if

I was going to cry the entire five minutes. I put on my big-girl undies and worked the process.

Chante Moore was my chosen R&B artist during Basic Training and Advanced Individual Training (AIT). I listened to her day and night so much so that I started thinking more and more about my husband. I decided to write him. I talked about how I missed him, but didn't miss his behaviors. If we were going to get back together, he was going to have to change. He promised that he would work on his anger and never put his hands on me again. We talked about getting a home; him requesting a duty station closer to our families; and having our own children. Our thoughts about having children who would be smart and athletic, like the two of us, blew our minds. Basic Training became easier to bear. Although we were apart, we had plans to get back together if things remained calm between us.

I was more willing to complete Basic and AIT. I worked hard every day so that I could be stronger mentally and physically. If nothing else, I was trained to use a deadly weapon and I was not afraid to use it.

December came, and I graduated from Basic and AIT. I felt new, and life was good – almost too good.

Six and I were making plans for his arrival back at his home station in Virginia. When he returned, I was there to greet him, and we had a wonderful weekend. I returned to Florida with the anticipation of moving back to Virginia with him.

Everything was going well for us. We were agreeing with each other and getting along, until we didn't. Although he didn't hit me, he talked baldly to me. I knew I must be crazy to sit and allow his behavior to continue after he promised that those days were behind us. But, the behavior was not. I decided to return to Florida to put an end to the relationship ... FOREVER.

Chapter 14

The Hard Part: Forgiving Me and Then Him

*"In order to heal, we must first forgive . . .
And, sometimes the person we must forgive
is ourselves". ~ Mila Bron*

When I returned home, I became employed as a correctional deputy. I worked at night, and decided that I would go to graduate school to become a mental health professional. Working nightly and going to school became taxing, and I really was not focusing on our relationship. Instead, I focused on taking care of myself and living life like I deserved. I started traveling and began seeing the world from a different perspective.

It was important for me to heal from the years of abuse, and not to blame others for the decisions I made. I said to myself numerous times that the only way I could heal was to forgive him. I never hated him for all that we endured, but I clearly had a lot of resentment. I felt broken. I thought that no one else would ever want me because I wasn't in a good mental state.

I wanted my healing process to begin. Therefore, I had to fully close the door on my relationship with Six, and I filed for a divorce. The divorce process itself was easy, but my emotional attachment held me back for months. Finally, I got the nerve to file the petition for divorce. When Six was home visiting, the process server attempted to serve him the divorce papers, but Six refused to sign them. Since Six was in the military, I was told that I couldn't file a default. Additional paperwork was required to ensure that I wasn't divorcing him without his knowledge. I researched what was required, paid all the fees, and had him served at the military base where he was stationed.

After being served, Six called to ask why I had him served at his job. I explained that for it to get approved, I had to serve him there because he had refused to sign when he was at home. He asked if I was sure that a divorce is what I wanted. I said, "Yes." He said he would sign the papers. I told him that he could call in on the day of the hearing if he didn't want to appear. He didn't appear or call in.

I officially closed that chapter of my life. I began to focus on forgiving me and moving forward to a healthier relationship. I saw Six maybe a few times over the next several years. Each encounter was very cordial. I had no fear of the unknown, no fear of him wanting to do harm to me anymore. I had one last conversation with him discussing the pain and foolishness that I endured when I was his wife. I apologized for not being who he needed me to be during that time. And, he apologized for abusing me and not knowing how to handle me with care. I accepted his apology. Then, it was on to living a healthy and happy life.

Chapter 15

Staying Free: Love Doesn't Hurt.

"Love doesn't hurt you. A person that doesn't know how to love hurts you.

Don't get it twisted." ~ Tony Gaskin

After being in a relationship for eleven years, which took most of my youth, it was difficult to move forward. Finding ways to not lose myself while being open to other relationships became difficult. I paid attention. I listened to how men looked at me and treated me. Did they value my voice or was I about to be in another abusive relationship? I was determined not to be a statistic or to find myself in another relationship that didn't support me moving towards a healthy and happy me. I kept reminding myself that love is never supposed to hurt. It is meant to breathe life into me. Since I experienced what I thought was love, but really wasn't, I was drawn to everything that was the opposite of what I had experienced.

To ensure that I didn't fall into brokenness, I paid attention to warning signs when I begin dating. I stopped caring about who people thought I should or shouldn't be dating. I listened to my inner critic, who was very critical of all my decisions. I questioned everyone's motives; I didn't know who I could trust.

Finding myself in a new relationship gave me the ability to love and trust again. I was going to be appreciated. I knew it wasn't going to be easy, but I was worth the try.

After the 9/11 attacks, I was on active duty. Six and I talked periodically. We saw each other a couple of times. Nothing about his presence made me want to ever consider having another relationship with him. We decided that we would be cordial and that we would at least speak to each other in passing. We had a past together, and no matter how painful it was, I had to honor it. Despite this truth, it didn't mean I needed to share a future with him.

I started speaking with young ladies about healthy relationships. When I had the opportunity to investigate cases of domestic violence, I always paid attention to the language that the victims were using and offered them comfort. I once was there too, and I survived. It became my responsibility to be an open book to those who were experiencing abuse. I became a vessel for understanding how the cycle of abuse occurs. I realized that I could help others see that although things might look good for a moment; the abuse would occur again when the anger regained strength.

I wanted families to know that it's not easy to just leave, and coming forward to admit the violence.. It can be life threatening. I was threatened numerous times by Six, and I believed him. In my case, I was the only one enduring the pain. Some victims have children, and the decision to leave is different for them. It was necessary for me to be a support to others even while I was still broken. I tried to find myself on the other side (bravery) and had the desire to help others.

When I remind victims that love doesn't hurt, I also remind myself that love doesn't hurt. I also deserve to be free from the bondage of the pain that I carried for so long.

"My Peace begins with me and it begins right now." ~ LaShonda Harolyn Henderson

Warning Signs

Many warning signs are subtle and easily missed. Dating and domestic violence can involve physical, sexual, and emotional abuse as well as threats. Although these are not all the warning signs that exists, these are the ones I ignored in my relationships.

1. He or she tries to isolate you from your family and friends. They are testing your loyalty and building your dependence on them.

2. He or she "play fight" with you. By play fighting, they are testing your limits to see how much you can and will tolerate.

3. He or she blames you for the arguments and never takes responsibility. They take the victim stance and never see their wrongs.

4. He or she is controlling. They want to know your every move. They want to know who

you are talking to, what you are wearing, and where you are at all time.

5. They are one way with you and another way with others. They go from being moody with you to being congenial around others.

6. He or She finds ways to put you down or disrespects you.

7. Lose temper over the smallest things like forgetting to buy ketchup.

8. If you feel like you are always walking on eggshells around him or her.

9. If he or she puts others down to build themselves up. They feel good about making others look bad.

10. If he or she doesn't like you working or makes multiple attempts to sabotage your current work situation

Family and Friends Can Help

There are some signs and symptoms of abuse that family and friends can look for when they feel like their love one might be in an abusive relationship. Recognizing the signs, you may be able to help them leave safely and begin the healing process.

1. When they are nervously anxious to please their partner.

2. Always agrees with their partner when their partner is clearly wrong.

3. They talk about the behaviors of the abuser.

4. The abuser is constantly calling and checking on their every move.

5. They have to explain bruises or is hiding the bruises with clothing that is not consistent with the weather.

6. They are restricted from seeing family and friends.

7. Low self-esteem when they use to be very confident.

8. They become depressed or suicidal.

9. Limited access to resources like their car, money, and house.

10. Frequently misses work, community activities, and family gatherings.

Resources for Victims and Their Families

Break the Cycle: www.breakthecycle.org

Center for Disease Control's Teen Dating Violence: www.cdc.gov

Florida Coalition Against Domestic Violence: www.fcadv.org

National Domestic Violence Hotline: 1-800-799-7233. www.hotline.org

National Teen Dating Abuse Hotline: 866-331-9474

National Youth Violence Prevention Resources Center: www.safeyouth.org

New Choices: www.newchoicesinc.org

Safe Space: www.safespace.org

That's Not Cool: www.thatsnotcool.com

WE-LEAP: https: www.we-leap2.com

Focus Group Questions

The Abuse:

According to the National Coalition Against Domestic Violence, 1 in 4 women and 1 in 9 men experience severe intimate partner physical violence, intimate partner contact sexual abuse violence, and/or intimate partner stalking with impacts such as injury, fearfulness, post-traumatic stress disorder, use of victim services, and contraction of sexual transmitted disease.

   a. Do you know someone who has been in an abusive situation?

   b. If yes, how did you come to know about the abuse?

   c. What did you do or say?

   d. How shocking are these statistics and what can we do to address this concern.

It's not just the Physical abuse:

1 in 15 children are exposed to intimate partner violence each year, and 90% of these children are eyewitnesses to this violence.

a. Can a "look" be emotional abuse?

b. Do you believe that children are affected by witnessing these events?

c. Can children be forced to "pick a side," when witnessing? Please share your reason for your answer.

What keeps her there:

Victims of intimate partner violence lose a total 8.0 million days of paid work each year.

a. Can constant criticism feel as if it is out of love and concern?

b. Can control appear gentle and kind?

c. Can women be financially and emotional tied to their abusers?

For Better (battered) or worst (death):

72% of all murder-suicides involve an intimate partner; 94% of the victims of these murder suicide are females.

a. Is leaving an abusive relationship a breaking of the marriage vows?

b. Should pastors address the problem of intimate dating violence?

c. How many sermons have you heard on domestic violence?

I'm just too young for this:

Women between the ages of 18-24 are most commonly abused by an intimate partner. Also intimate partner violence is linked to adolescent pregnancy, unintended pregnancy and miscarriages. Nearly 1.5 million high school students in the United States are physically abused by dating partners every year.

a. Can you imagine your child, niece, cousin, or someone you loved involved in intimate dating violence?

b. What advice would you give her?

c. How can you support her through this tough time?

I need a plan:

1 in 7 women and 1 in 18 men have been stalked by an intimate partner during their lifetime to the point in which they felt very fearful or believed that they or someone close to them would be harmed or killed.

a. How hard is it to walk away from something you love and are accustom to?

b. Have you ever encouraged someone to leave? How did you assist with that plan?

c. What advice would you give someone who was trying to leave, and they knew it will likely not end well.

A new way of thinking:

43% of dating college women reported experiencing abusive behaviors from their partner.

a. How can we teach the young to speak up and speak out?

b. Where and with whom do young boys/girls learn to respect each?

c. Where are the resources in your community for intimate dating victims?

A Time to heal:

Studies suggest that there is a relationship between intimate partner violence and depression and suicidal behaviors.

a. How does intimate dating violence affects our faith?

b. How do we reassure the survival that they did nothing wrong?

c. How does healing look to you?

Longest walk home:

The cost of intimate partner violence exceeds 8.3 billion a year. What is your peace worth to you?

a. What can women learn from other women about moving from victim to survival?

b. How can we support survivals of intimate partner violence in maintaining healthy relationships and healing?

c. How can we create an environment where people feel free to be honest?

Afterword

It might be the end of this book, but it's just the start of our relationship. Let's stay in contact. I really want to know how you are doing with finding and maintaining healthy relationships. I'm always interested in helping others through the process of creating healthy relationships.

Do you need a powerful speaker who can motivate, inspire, and energize your organization, staff, or group? If so, I have a unique ability to connect to an audience. Drawing from my experiences as a mental health counselor and a trauma survivor, my message gets right to the point and to the heart of these issues.

My story is unforgettable. My message is invaluable. I provide keynote addresses and workshops that make a lasting effect on the lives of my audiences.

Office: 772-242-3298

Fax: 772-618-6585

Website: www.talktherapywithlashonda.com

Email: Talktherapywithlashonda@gmail.com

Social Sites: Facebook, LinkedIn, Instagram

About the Author

LaShonda Harolyn Henderson is a Licensed Mental Health Counselor and owner of L&L Clinical Counseling Services, LLC. With more than eighteen years of professional mental health experience, LaShonda specializes in treating individuals with trauma and those who engage in high-risk activities like self-injurious behaviors and substance abuse.

A native of Fort Pierce, LaShonda earned a master's degree in community mental health from Webster University and a bachelor's degree in sociology from Old Dominion University. She also holds certifications as a Master's Level Certified Addiction Professional and a Certified Clinical Trauma Professional.

For the past twenty years, LaShonda has been a proud member of Zeta Phi Beta Sorority, Incorporated and currently serves as the President of Zeta Eta Zeta Chapter in Fort Pierce. A passionate community activist and voice for the voiceless, LaShonda works diligently to create change in her community. She is one of the founding members of the Lincoln Park

Young Professionals, a group of community change agents who serve and advocate for the Lincoln Park community.

LaShonda is also a member of a host of professional and community organizations including We-LEAP, Inc., a nonprofit organization providing domestic violence awareness and advocacy services, where she serves as a board member.

When LaShonda is not hard at work in the community, she encourages others to live the best life possible.

In her spare time, she enjoys traveling the world, crafting, and reading a good book.

Made in the USA
Columbia, SC
14 February 2019